Pebble® Bilingüe/Bilingual Plus

Mira dentro/Look Inside

Mira dentro de un tipi

Look Inside a Tepee

por/by Mari Schuh

Editora consultora/Consulting Editor: Gail Saunders-Smith, PhD

Consultor/Consultant: Dr. Troy Johnson, Director/Chair
Estudios de Indios Americanos/American Indian Studies
California State University, Long Beach

CAPSTONE PRESS
a capstone imprint

Pebble Plus is published by Capstone Press,
151 Good Counsel Drive, P.O. Box 669, Mankato, Minnesota 56002.
www.capstonepub.com

Books published by Capstone Press are manufactured with paper
containing at least 10 percent post-consumer waste.

Library of Congress Cataloging-in-Publication Data
Schuh, Mari C., 1975–
  [Look inside a tepee. Spanish & English]
  Mira dentro de un tipi = Look inside a tepee / por Mari Schuh.
    p. cm.—(Pebble plus bilingüe/bilingual. Mira dentro/Look inside)
  Includes index.
  Summary: "Simple text and photographs present tepees, their construction, and their interaction with the
environment—in both English and Spanish"—Provided by publisher.
  ISBN 978-1-4296-6911-5 (library binding)
  1. Tipis—Juvenile literature. I. Title. II. Title: Look inside a tepee.
  E98.D8S38 2012
  690'.8'08997—dc22   2011000657

Editorial Credits
Megan Peterson, editor; Strictly Spanish, translation services; Renée T. Doyle, designer; Danielle Ceminsky,
    bilingual book designer; Wanda Winch, media researcher; Laura Manthe, production specialist

Photo Credits
Alamy/Megapress, 9; North Wind Picture Archives/Nancy Carter, 13
iStockphoto/C. L. Kunst, 15; Eric Foltz, 5; Mark Murphy, 24
Nativestock.com/Marilyn Angel Wynn, 7, 21
North Wind Picture Archives/Nancy Carter, 11, 17, 19
Shutterstock/Judy Crawford, 1, 22–23; South12th Photography, back cover, 3; Todd Pierson, front cover

Note to Parents and Teachers

The Mira dentro/Look Inside set supports national social studies standards related to
people, places, and culture. This book describes and illustrates tepees in both English and
Spanish. The images support early readers in understanding the text. The repetition of
words and phrases helps early readers learn new words. This book also introduces early
readers to subject-specific vocabulary words, which are defined in the Glossary section.
Early readers may need assistance to read some words and to use the Table of Contents,
Glossary, Internet Sites, and Index sections of the book.

Printed in the United States of America in North Mankato, Minnesota.
032011
006110CGF11

Table of Contents

Tabla de contenidos

What Is a Tepee?

A tepee is a tent made of
wood poles and buffalo hides.
The Plains Indians once lived
in tepees.

¿Qué es un tipi?

Un tipi es una carpa hecha
de postes de madera y pieles
de búfalo. Hace tiempo, los
indios de las llanuras vivían
en tipis.

5

The Plains Indians moved from place to place to hunt buffalo. Tepees were easy to take down and move.

_____

Los indios de las llanuras se mudaban de un lugar a otro para cazar búfalos. Los tipis eran fáciles de desarmar y mover.

6

7

Building a Tepee

Plains Indian women built the tepee. They tied poles together to form a cone.

Cómo construir un tipi

Las indias de las llanuras construían el tipi. Ellas ataban postes juntos para formar un cono.

9

Plains Indian women

fit buffalo hides

over the poles.

Las indias de las llanuras

colocaban pieles de búfalo

sobre los postes.

10

Logs or stones held the tepee
to the ground. The tepee
door faced east to greet
the morning sun.

Troncos o piedras sostenían al
tipi en el suelo. La puerta del
tipi enfrentaba el este para
saludar al sol de la mañana.

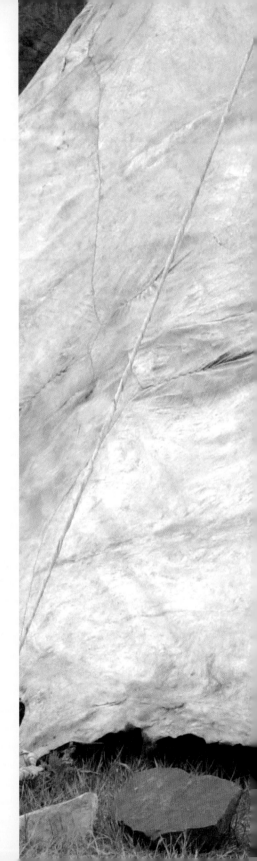

13

Inside a Tepee

The Plains Indians made a fire in the middle of the tepee. A hole at the top of the tepee let out smoke.

Dentro de un tipi

Los indios de las llanuras encendían una fogata en el medio del tipi. Un agujero en la punta del tipi permitía salir el humo.

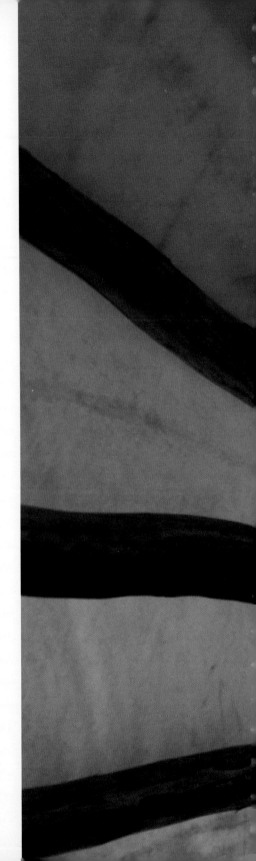

In winter, thick buffalo hides
lined the inside of the tepee.
The hides kept out the wind.
In summer, the bottom of the
tepee was rolled up.

En invierno, pieles gruesas de
búfalos cubrían el interior del
tipi. Las pieles no dejaban que
entrara el viento. En el verano,
la parte inferior del tipi era
enrollada hacia arriba.

buffalo hide/piel de búfalo

17

The Plains Indians slept
under furs and blankets.
Tools and supplies hung
on the tepee's walls.

Los indios de las llanuras
dormían bajo pieles y
mantas. Las herramientas
y las provisiones colgaban
de las paredes.

Tepees Today

Today the Plains Indians use tepees for ceremonies. They also use tepees to learn about the past.

Los tipis hoy

Hoy, los indios de las llanuras usan los tipis para ceremonias. Ellos usan los tipis también para aprender acerca del pasado.

Glossary

buffalo—a large animal with a big, hairy head, a humped back, and short horns, found in North America

ceremony—special actions, words, or music performed to mark an important event

cone—an object or shape with a round base and a point at the top

hide—the skin of an animal; many buffalo hides were sewn together to make a tepee cover; when there were fewer buffalo, tepees were made of strong cloth called canvas

Plains Indians—Native Americans who lived in the Great Plains of the United States and Canada

Internet Sites

FactHound offers a safe, fun way to find Internet sites related to this book. All of the sites on FactHound have been researched by our staff.

Here's all you do:

Visit *www.facthound.com*

Type in this code: 9781429669115

Super-cool stuff! Check out projects, games and lots more at **www.capstonekids.com**

22

Glosario

el búfalo—un animal grande con una cabeza grande y peluda, una espalda jorobada y cuernos cortos, encontrado en América del Norte

la ceremonia—acciones, palabras y música especiales que se realizan para marcar un evento importante

el cono—un objeto o forma con una base redonda que termina en punta

los indios de las llanuras—nativoamericanos que vivían en las Grandes Llanuras de Estados Unidos y Canadá

la piel—la piel de un animal; muchas pieles de búfalo se cosían juntas para hacer una cubierta para el tipi; cuando los búfalos no eran tan numerosos, los tipis estaban hechos de una tela resistente llamada lona

Sitios de Internet

FactHound brinda una forma segura y divertida de encontrar sitios de Internet relacionados con este libro. Todos los sitios en FactHound han sido investigados por nuestro personal.

Esto es todo lo que tienes que hacer:

Visita *www.facthound.com*

Ingresa este código: 9781429669115

¡Algo súper divertido! Hay proyectos, juegos y mucho más en www.capstonekids.com

23

Index

buffalo, 4, 6, 10, 16
ceremonies, 20
cones, 8
doors, 12
fires, 14
hides, 4, 10, 16
hunting, 6
logs, 12
moving, 6

poles, 4, 8, 10
sleeping, 18
stones, 12
summer, 16
tents, 4
tools, 18
winter, 16
women, 8, 10

Índice

búfalo, 4, 6, 10, 16
carpas, 4
cazar, 6
ceremonias, 20
conos, 8
dormir, 18
fogata, 14
herramientas, 18
indias, 8, 10

invierno, 16
mudar, 6
piedras, 12
pieles, 4, 10, 16
postes, 4, 8, 10
puertas, 12
troncos, 12
verano, 16